MW01711167

# Contemplating Compassion:

## A Compilation of Quotations Designed to Encourage Reflection and to Promote Mindfulness

*Frontispiece: By the Speaking of this Truth*

# Contemplating Compassion:

## A Compilation of Quotations Designed to Encourage Reflection and to Promote Mindfulness

Compiled and illustrated by

Steven L. Berg, PhD

EHIPASSIKO PRESS

*Ehipassiko:* Encouraging Investigation

Farmington Hills, Michigan
2024

Ehipassiko Press

2024

In the spirit of Open Educational Resources (OERs) and of not charging for the *dhamma*, we have priced the paperback edition of this book at cost of production. Neither the author nor publisher receive any royalties or other compensation for the sale of this book. Free .pdf files of the book are available online at ehipassikopress.org.

This book is licensed under a Creative Commons Attribution-NonCommerical-ShareAlike 4.0 International License.

© 2024 Ehipassiko Press, LLC

ISBN: 978-1-962024-09-9

# Dedication

To the Congregation at

The Great Lakes Buddhist Vihara
Livonia, Michigan

# Contents

Acknowledgements

*Ehipassiko Press' business model has no income stream. Copies of our books are made available online for free. Paperback editions are sold through Amazon at cost of production. Neither our authors nor Ehipassiko Press receive any royalties or other compensation. All books are published at a financial loss. Therefore, we are especially grateful to the following individuals without whose contributions this book would not have been published.*

In addition to the members of the Great Lakes Buddhist Vihara, I am especially grateful to Bhanthe Venerable Yatinuwara Sankichcha Thero and to the Venerable Brahmanagama Muditha Nayaka Thero who have provided me with dhamma instruction for the past 17 years. They, and many other monks associated with the vihara have influenced me greatly.

I would like to highlight one act of compassion that happened shortly after I began to regularly attend the Great Lakes Buddhist Vihara. After the congregation chanted the Five Precepts, Chandratilaka leaned over and said, "Your Pali is getting very good." At that moment, I truly felt that I was a member of the community. Since then, Chandrtilaka and her husband Chandrapala have become friends and mentors.

Among my valued colleagues at Schoolcraft College, I am grateful to Kim Lark, Josselyn Moore, Jessica Worden-Jones, and Brett Griffiths.

I want to acknowledge the support I receive from Chilan Sethuge as well as dhamma friends who attend Saturday meditation and tea. I am especially grateful to Jackson Knapp.

Dr. Steven Fischer continues to make an important contribution to my physical, mental, and spiritual development.

# Introduction

---

*Steve sponsored the Kathina all by himself—with the help of the community.*

---

In 2009, I sponsored the Kathina ceremony at the Great Lakes Buddhist Vihara, the first Westerner to do so at this primarily Sri Lankan temple. This ceremony marks the end of the three month retreat taken by monastics in Sri Lanka and other countries that practice Theravada Buddhism. Generally, as part of the ceremony, new robes and other gifts are given to monks and nuns.

Since then, Bhanthe Sankichcha has often remarked that "Steve sponsored the Kathina all by himself—with the help of the community."

In 2024, I again have the privilege to sponsor Kathina. Again, it would be impossible for me to carry out my responsibilities without community support. To show my appreciation for this support, I compiled the quotations in this book as a gift to the community who supported me. I am sharing it with others who are interested in contemplating compassion regardless of the worldview that informs their life choices.

*Contemplating Compassion* is not a Buddhist book in that I am not attempting to teach about Buddhism. I do not write "Buddhist" books. Although, my worldview is strongly influenced by my Theravada Buddhist practice, my research and writing reflect my interdisciplinary academic practice of drawing on a variety of seemingly unrelated sources to investigate topics in new ways. As a result, the quotations in this book range from formal commentary about the Buddha dhamma to the study of bacteria and Charles Darwin's *The Descent of Man*.

The quotations include scripture from a variety of religious and philosophical traditions as well as commentary from Buddhist monks, lay people, and academics who study compassion. Most of the texts I selected might not be familiar to most readers. And that is the point. I want to challenge readers to consider the role of compassion in their lives from new perspectives.

Although *Contemplating Compassion* is designed to be read from beginning to end over the course of 31 days, it need not be used that way. You can read multiple entries a day or spread the reading out for more than a month. You don't even need to read the book in order.

Regardless of how you use *Contemplating Compassion* for reflection, I hope that you will benefit from this unique approach to contemplating this important topic.

Steven L. Berg, PhD
Professor of English and History
Schoolcraft College

# Beginning the Month

A small teaching technique that educators use is to ask students to predict what is being covered in a book, article, or lecture before they begin reading it. Regardless of whether students are correct, they learn more because they have stimulated their previous knowledge on the topic.

*What do I predict will be covered in a book called* Contemplating Compassion*? What would I include in such a book?*

*Veneration of the 28 Buddhas*

## Day 1

**Reflecting on and recollecting the Buddha, Dhamma, and Sangha as refuges is always an important reminder for us. The reality is that we are always taking refuge in something, whether it is in some distraction or particular worry or fear. The mind goes there, and that's where we create our refuge. We rely on it and build our lives around it. As we find out, that's not a very satisfying refuge, but it's what we do as human beings.**

Pasanno, Bhikkhu. *Abundant, Exalter, Immeasurable.* Abhayagiri Buddhist Monastery, 2016. p. 2.

*What are some of the things in which I take refuge? On what things do I build my life around?*

FIG. 16.
PROBOSCIS OF BLOW-FLY.
× 40.

[*to face page* 71.

*Proboscis of Blow-Fly*

# Day 2

**Make haste slowly. Make your effort consistent and steady. Give yourself time to incorporate the meditation practice into your life, and let your practice grow gradually and gently.**

Gunaratana, Bhante. *Mindfulness in Plain English*. 2002. Wisdom, 2019. p. 77.

*In what ways do I want to rush my Buddhist practice or other aspects of my life? About what do I feel impatient and why do I feel this way? Am I concerned, troubled, mystified, impatient that it is already the second day of the month and the word "compassion" has not appeared in either of the first two quotations?*

*Fighting Our Internal Demons*

## Day 3

**We all have the tendency to run away from suffering. But the fact is that without suffering, there is no way to cultivate understanding and compassion. I don't want to send my friends and children to a place without suffering, because a place without suffering is a place without understanding and compassion. Without understanding and compassion, there is no happiness.**

Hahn, Thich Nhat. *Breath, You Are Alive!: Sutra on the Full Awareness of Breathing*. 1990. Parallax Press, 2008. p. 4.

*What do I lose when I try to flee from suffering? In what ways have I used my own suffering to gain more compassion for others? Although we do not wish suffering on ourselves or others, how has suffering lead to an increase in happiness for me and the people around me?*

*Sitting with Centipedes*

## Day 4

**Thus the entire process of training in the Dhamma is rooted in personal experience. Even faith should be rooted in investigation and inquiry and not based solely upon emotional leanings and blind belief. Faith alone is insufficient but is the door to deeper levels of experience. Faith serves as a spur to practice; practice leads to experiential understanding; and when one's understanding matures, it blossoms in full realization.**

Bodhi, Bhikkhu. *In the Buddha's Words: An Anthology of Discourses from the Pali Canon.* Wisdom, 2005. p. 87.

*Are there times when I have exhibited a blind faith? Have I focused too much on reading or reciting suttas than I have in investigating my experience and how it can help me better understand suttas? Are there times when I find it easier to recite the Karaniya Metta Sutta than in practicing it? How does my experience with compassion help me better understand the Karaniya Metta Sutta?*

*The Creation of Light*

# Day 5

**Nevertheless, it is important to avoid associating spiritual progress with a particular sitting posture. What counts, in the end, is the condition of the mind.**

Analayo, Bhikkhu. *Mindfulness of Breathing: A Practice Guide and Translations*. Wildhorse Publications, 2019. p. 13.

*What is the condition of my mind at this moment? Do I have a special time of day or place where I practice meditation? Do I join others for meditation? Have I experimented with different postures or types of meditation?*

# The Meaning of Compassion

During the first part of the month, we laid a foundation for reflection. We considered why and how we meditate and reflect. During the next few days, we will consider what we mean when we talk about compassion/*karuna*.

If you do research on compassion in a Western, academic context, you will find that there are many definitions of compassion. Some are better than others to use in understanding Buddhist practice. *Contemplating Compassion* will not attempt to provide a “correct” definition. Instead, it will invite you to use your experience to reflect on the meaning of compassion in your life and the lives of others. But first you should consider what you think about, what you mean, when you say “compassion.”

*What does compassion mean to me? How would I define it? How do I recognize it in others? How do I recognize it in myself?*

*Protecting Others While Protecting Ourselves*

# Day 6

**Etymologically, the word [compassion] is derived from the roots *com* meaning "together" and *pati* meaning "to suffer." To have compassion means that you are in solidarity with those who are suffering.,.. In fact, true compassion means that one is suffering with the other.**

Poppo, Kristin. "A Pedagogy of Compassion: Janusz Karczak and the Care of the Child." *Encounter: Education for Meaning and Social Justice,* vol. 19, no. 4, 2006, pp. 32-39. p. 33.

*What does it mean to suffer with someone? Do I have to literally feel their suffering in the same way that they are feeling it to offer compassion to them? How can I show my solidarity with someone who is suffering in my household? In my community? In my country? In other parts of the world?*

*Untitled*

# Day 7

**We define compassion as simply being moved in our depths by other's experiences and responding to a way that intends to ease their suffering or promote their flourishing.**

Rogers, Jr., Frank. *Compassion in Practice: The Way of Jesus*. Upper Room, 2016. p. 30.

*Is there value in reading commentary from non-Buddhist sources? Why or why not? How can reading a Christian definition of compassion help me better understand the Buddha Dhamma? Must we respond to someone or can we just feel compassion for them?*

*Famine Among Plenty*

# Day 8

**Karuna is also closely connected to the four noble truths. Accordingly, the compassionate sees the pain and suffering of others (*dukkha*), the reason for such suffering (*dukkha Samudaya),* the solution to the problem of suffering (*eightfold path*), and the motivation for such compassion is the desire for other people to be relieved of suffering (*Nirvana*).**

Augustine, Parattukudi. "Understanding the Phenomenon: A Comparative Study of Compassion of the West and *Karuna* of the East." *Asian Philosophy*, vol. 29, no. 1, 2019, pp. 1-19. p. 13. Citing Anallayo, B. (2015). *Compassion and Emptiness in Buddhist Meditation*. Cambridge: Windhorse Publications.

*What are examples from my experience that demonstrate how an understanding of the Four Noble Truths can help me better understand suffering in others? How does this understanding help me show compassion to others? Can I use my Buddhist understanding of the dukkha and the Four Noble Truths to help non-Buddhists relieve suffering in their lives? What are skillful ways that I can attempt to do this?*

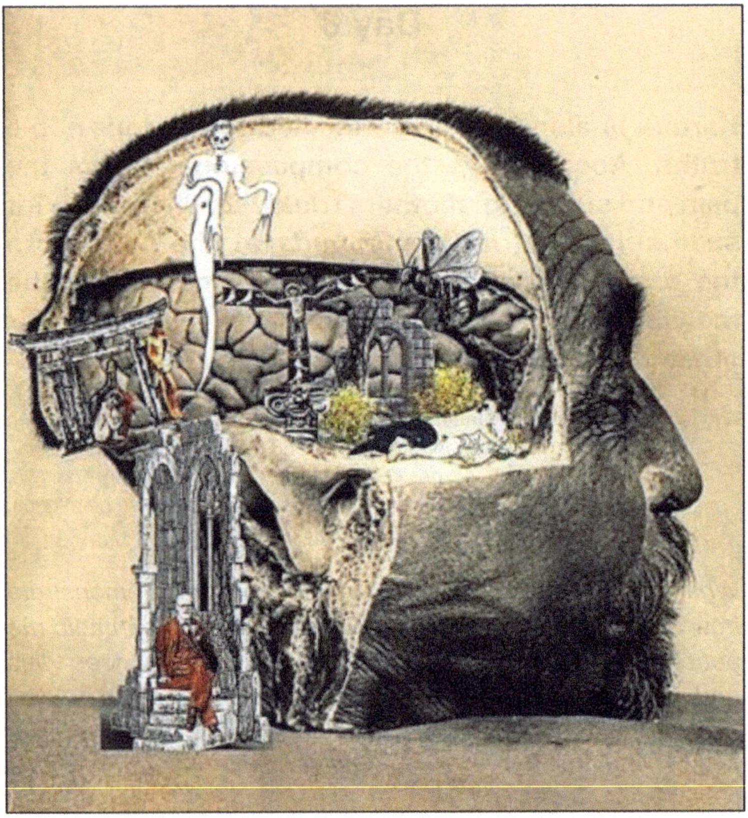

*Psychoanthropology*

# Day 9

**In practice, prajna [wisdom] gives rise to karuna [compassion], and karuna gives rise to prajna. Truly, you can't have one without the other.**

O'Brien, Barbara. "Buddhism and Compassion." *Learning Religion*. 9 Jul. 2018. www.learnreligions.com/buddhism-and-compassion-449719

*How do I see the relationship between wisdom and compassion? What types of wisdom am I learning by what I read, what study? With what am I filling my mind by the types of choices I make and actions I take? Am I focused on learning wise, skillful, or right wisdom?*

*For Finch*

# Day 10

**It is compassion that compels one to serve others with altruistic motives. A truly compassionate person lives with altruistic motives. A truly compassionate person lives not for himself but for others. He seeks opportunities to serve others expecting nothing in return, not even gratitude.**

Narada. *The Buddha and His Teachings*. 1964. Buddhist Missionary Society, 1988. p. 629.

*What is the root cause of the negativities that arise when someone does not show "appropriate" gratitude when I act with compassion? Are there times when my compassionate acts are really centered on promoting myself and not assisting others? In what ways have I shown my gratitude when others have acted compassionately toward me?*

*Trinity of Madonnas with Children*

# Day 11

**Buddhist compassion is the result of knowing one is part of a greater whole and is interdependent and connected to that whole…. The more one reads Buddhist writings, the more one realizes that Buddhist compassion is similar to lay conceptions of compassion in name only. While lay concepts of compassion are of warm feelings for particular people in need, Buddhist compassion is not particular, warm, or even a feeling.**

Goetz, Jennifer. "Research on Buddhist Conceptions of Compassion: An Annotated Bibliography." *Greater Good Science Center*." 1 Jun. 2004. greatergood.berkeley.edu/article/item/buddhist_conceptions_of_compassion_an_annotated_bibliography.

*In what ways am I interdependent on people whom I have never met? How do these people impact the quality of my life? In what ways do my actions impact people in other cities, states, countries? In what ways do I feel empathy for people whom I do not know? How do I change those feelings of empathy into acts of compassion?*

# The Evolutionary Origins of Compassion

When most people consider the theory of evolution, their first thought is the phrase "survival of the fittest." Yet, this phrase does not appear in any of Charles Darwin's books, journals, or letters. Darwin instead wrote that *sympathy* is the basic building block of evolution. Where he writing in the twenty-first century instead of the nineteenth century, he might have phrased his argument as "survival of the compassionate." Although Darwin acknowledges that on an individual level, it is the fittest who survive. But a species that acts with compassion is most likely to survive. We survive best when we realize that we are interdependent and connected.

By observing evolutionary factors, we learn that there can be a cost to an individual who is acting with compassion. Even in bacterial communities, there is evidence of individuals who are willing to sacrifice themselves for the benefit of the community.

*What might be the costs to me of living a compassionate life? These could be costs in terms of time, money, relationships, self-view. What are the benefits of living a compassionate life? These can be in terms of myself, my family, my community, my world.*

*St. Francis*

## Day 12

**For with those animals which were benefited by living in close association, the individuals which took the greatest pleasure in society would best escape various dangers; while those that cared least for their comrades and lived solitary would perish in greater numbers. ... In however complex a manner this feeling may have originated, as it is one of high importance to all those animals which aid and defend each other, it will have been increased, through natural selection; for those communities which included the greatest number of the most sympathetic members, would flourish best and rear the greatest number of offspring.**

Darwin, Charles. *The Decent of Man, and the Selection in Relation to Sex.* vol. 1. New York, 1872. p. 77, 79.

*In what ways do I benefit from being part of a community? How do I survive better because other people show me compassion? How to I help others survive better by showing them compassion?*

*Active Learning*

# Day 13

**It should be no surprise, given Darwin's commitment to the continuity of species, that he would claim that concern for the welfare of others is not a uniquely human characteristic.**

Ekman, Paul. "Darwin's Compassionate View of Human Nature." *JAMA*, vol. 303, no. 6, Feb. 2010, p. 557. DOI: doi.org/10.1001/jama.2010.101. p. 557.

*What can I learn about compassion from non-human animals such as a beloved pet? Other domesticated animals? Animals who have not been domesticated? How have non-human animals shown me compassion? How have I shown non-human animals compassion? Can I share the same types of compassion with other humans?*

*The Dhamma of Accharomyces Cerevisiae*

# Day 14

**Microorganisms have been cooperating with each other for billions of years: by sharing resources, communicating with each other, and joining together to form biofilms and other large structures. These cooperative behaviors benefit the colony as a whole; however, they may be costly to the individuals performing them.**

Allen, Benjamin and Martin A. Nowak. "Cooperation and the Fate of Microbial Societies." *PLoS Biology,* vol. 11, no. 4, 2013, pp. 1-3. DOI: 10.1371/journal.pbio.1001549.

*What are some of the costs associated with acts of compassion that I have performed? Were there costs that I did not anticipate? What does the concept of self-sacrifice mean to me? How do I practice self-sacrifice skillfully?*

*Persimmons and Poetry*

## Day 15

**The trees in a forest care for each other, sometimes even going so far as to nourish the stump of a felled tree for centuries after it was cut down by feeding it sugars and other nutrients, and so keeping it alive.**

Wohlleben, Peter. *The Hidden Lives of Trees: What They Feel and How They Communicate*. Greystone, 2016. p. viii.

*Who are the stumps in my life whom I continue to nourish? Have there been times—even brief periods of time such as brought on by illness--where I have been a "stump," someone dependent on others for my survival? Because I am aware that I am subject to old age, sickness, and death, have I prepared for the day when I become a stump?*

*Gorilla Dhamma*

# Day 16

**Casual actions are often sufficient to alert the gorillas and to make them uneasy. For example, I believe that even the possession of a firearm is sufficient to imbue one's behavior with a certain unconscious aggressiveness, a feeling of being superior, which an animal can detect. When meeting a gorilla face to face, I reasoned, an attack would be more likely if I carried a gun than if I simply showed my apprehension and uncertainty.**

Schaller, George B. *The Year of the Gorilla*. University of Chicago Press, 1964. p. 112-113.

*When have I been unconsciously aggressive or shown feelings of superiority toward others? How do these feelings of aggression and superiority impact my ability to act with compassion toward others?*

## The Importance of Self Compassion

When we practice Metta meditation, we begin with ourselves and then radiate our loving kindness outward. We wish that "In gladness and in safety, May all beings be at ease." We do not distinguish whether they are weak or strong, seen or unseen, living near or far, born or unborn. We omit no one.

Too often, in our efforts to act with compassion to others, we forget to treat ourselves with compassion. But, if we don't take care of ourselves, we have nothing to offer others.

*In what ways do I currently show myself compassion?*

*The Story of the Lotus*

# Day 17

**In Thailand the rafters in the Dhamma Hall are great territory for wandering geckos. If a monk gets annoyed because he chooses to sit under the rafters and the geckos defecate on him, whose problem is that?**

Amaro, Ajahn. "Pesky Woodpeckers," *Beginning Our Day*, vol. 2, Abhayagiri Buddhist Monastery, 2015. p. 122.

*When have I sat under the equivalent of defecating geckos? Why didn't I move? Why do I sometimes find it difficult to take care of myself? Do I consider myself selfish or not living the spirit of the Buddha Dhamma if I act on my needs?*

*Public Health*

## Day 18

**They [teachers] are repeatedly told how important they are and how they should prioritize their well-being, and then asked to do the exact opposite.... Administrators or peers impressed with our dedication or commiserating in good-natured ways about the lack of time for ourselves can make it hard to see just how unhealthy these practices become when they become an expected and accepted part of the way teachers work.**

Cruz, Colleene. *Risk. Fail. Rise: A Teacher's Guide to Learning From* Mistakes. Heinemann, 2021. Excerpt Reprinted in Nimah Gobir.. "Why Setting Boundaries is Helpful for Teachers and Their Students." *Mind/Shift*. 6 Apr. 2021. www.kqed.org/mindshift/57540/why-setting-boundaries-is-helpful-for-teachers-and-their-students.

*Do I ever take pride in the fact that I am too busy? In what ways are the people with whom I work—bosses, peers, subordinates—impressed with my dedication? When is this dedication a result of skillful actions? When is this dedication a result of unhealthy practices? In what ways can I begin to change these unhealthy practices so that I can show myself compassion?*

*The Temptation of Mara*

# Day 19

**Although it may not be obvious at first glance, self-compassion plays a key role in the quest to end sexism, racism, heterosexism, and other forms of oppression. By aiming compassion inward as well as outward, we can better confront the pain of injustice without being overwhelmed, and find the strength and energy to fight for what's right.**

Neff, Kristen. "Four Ways Self Compassion Can Help You Fight for Social Justice." *Greater Good Magazine*. 14 Jun. 2021. greatergood.berkeley.edu/article/item/four_ways_self_compassion_can_help_you_fight_for_social_justice.

*Are there times that I feel overwhelmed by the injustice in my personal life or in the world? From where do these feelings arise? How does taking care of myself make it easier for me to fight against injustice, to fight for what's right? What is one specific thing I can do today to help me show myself compassion?*

# Living a Life of Compassion

Compassion is not an isolated act or a series of isolated acts that we take. We need to move toward having a lifestyle of compassion.

*How do I currently incorporate acts of compassion into my daily life? How is acting with compassion part of my lifestyle? Are there certain compassionate acts that I take on a regular basis?*

*Use Every Moment to the Best of Your Ability*

# Day 20

**How do I decide what to do? Simply put, I try to make kind choices; I try to increase compassion and reduce cruelty.**

Berkoff, Marc. *The Emotional Lives of Animals*. New World Library, 2002. p. 164.

*What do I consider when deciding whether a choice is kind or not? What criteria do I use when deciding to act with kindness? When do I mistake cruelty for kindness such as when I am motivated by anger to tell someone something for their own good?*

*Don't Stress*

## Day 21

**The path of developing loving-kindness and compassion is to be patient with the fact that you're human and that you make these mistakes. That's more important than getting it right.**

Chodron, Pema. "The Answer to Anger and Aggression is Patience." *Lion's Roar.* www.lionsroar.com/the-answer-to-anger-aggression-is-patience.

*In what ways am I my own worst critic when it comes to errors? Do I hold myself to an unrealistic standard of perfection? When do I blow my errors and mistakes out of proportion? Do I ever use "I am just human" as an excuse for not accepting responsibility for my mistakes?*

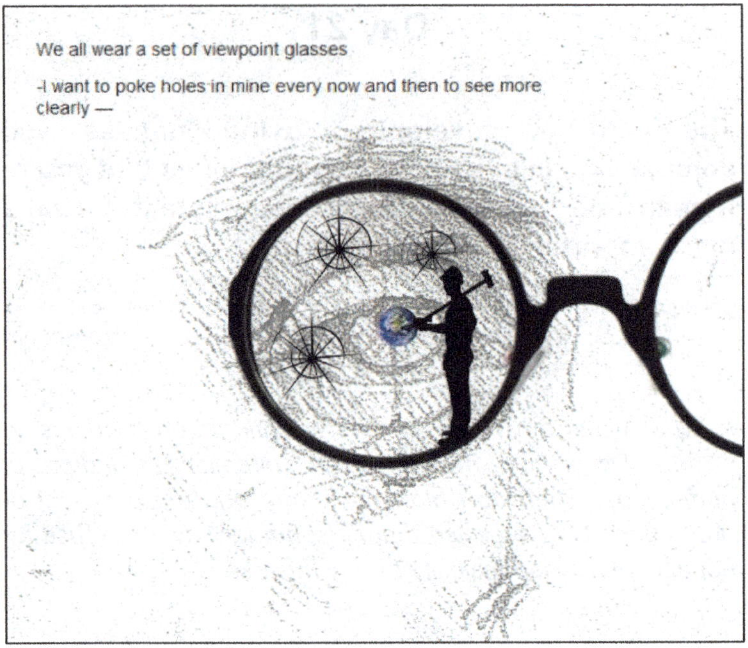


*Seeing More Clearly*

# Day 22

**It's hard to let go of the belief that our homes need to be picture-perfect — or maybe I should say "Pinterest-perfect" — before we can welcome guests over. But the idea that we must make our home look un-lived in before having people over stops so many of us from sharing life together.**

Shreeves, Robin. "In Praise of 'Scruffy Hospitality.'" *Treehugger*. 17 Jun. 2019. www.treehugger.com/in-priase-scruffy-hospitality-4868485.

*Are there times when I have not shared my life with someone else because it is not perfect? Because I want to hide my humanness from them? Are there times when I have not been able to receive compassionate assistance from others because I present my life as being perfectly tidy? What are ways that I prevent myself from sharing my life with others or for them to share their lives with me?*

## Acting Compassionately Toward Others

Compassion is not a feeling. We feel empathy. Compassion is an action. Our feelings of empathy compel us to act with compassion.

Although acting compassionately toward ourselves serves as a foundation for Buddhist practice, our goal in living lives of compassion is to serve others. As Charles Darwin demonstrated, we survive best in a compassionate community. As the Gautama Buddha taught in the *Karaniya Metta Sutta*:

> So with a boundless heart
>     Should one cherish all living beings;
> Radiating kindness over the entire world:
>     Spreading upwards to the skies,
> And downwards to the depths;
>     Outwards and unbounded,
> Freed from hatred and ill-will.

*In what ways is metta (loving-kindness) a basis for compassionate actions? What is the difference between metta and karuna (compassion)?*

*Humanity at the Front Line*

## Day 23

**Where can we start [to show compassion]? One place to begin is to look for opportunities for small acts of kindness in ordinary places. Sometimes something as simple as a smile, a warm gaze, or a small gesture can go a long way.**

Kurland, Beth. "Beyond Empathy: The Power of Compassion." *Psychology Today*. 18 Sept. 2019. www.psychologytoday.com/us/blog/the-well-being-toolkit/201909/beyond-empathy-the-power-compassion.

*In what ways have I already been presented with opportunities to show compassion today? Have I taken them? Why or why not? What is a small gesture I took yesterday that can be considered an act of compassion? When did someone make a small gesture that you found to be compassionate?*

*Earthworm Kindness*

# Day 24

**Like all relationships, those we have with our companions here require our generosity, and we have to put our hearts into that. We do this by opening our eyes, taking a look around, seeing how people are doing, and responding with our hearts. We reach out to people who look like they may be struggling, not doing so well, or needing a little bit of a lift. And in our hearts, we forgive those who've made mistakes, whether they've asked for forgiveness or not. That's just ordinary kindness, but it's earthworm kindness—it's what creates an environment in the community that is very beautiful and uplifting. It provides the tilled soil from which fertility, growth, and development of individuals can take place.**

Yatiko, Ajahn. "Two Kinds of Fools," *Beginning Our Day*, vol. 2, Abhayagiri Buddhist Monastery, 2015. p. 73.

*In what ways do I practice earthworm kindness? Is there anyone to whom I feel angry? Can I forgive them? Do I realize that forgiving someone's actions is not the same as saying that they should not be held accountable for their actions? How does forgiving others improve my life? How have I recently tilled the soil in someone else's life through an act of compassion? How did this act of compassion build community or help them grow?*

*Offering Dhamma*

## Day 25

**But developing a sense of community demands we cultivate friendships with people we might not choose ordinarily. And founding friendships on *commitment* rather than "chemistry" often requires adjustment but can give a different meaning to our lives and our work.**

Siddiqui, Mona. "Divine Welcome: The Ethics of hospitality in Islam and Christianity." *ABC Religion and Ethics*. 29 Jul. 2020. www.abc.net.au/religion/mona-siddiqui-hospitality-as-welcoming-in-gods-name/12503800.

*How do I see the difference between commitment and chemistry? In what ways can relying on chemistry to build relationships be a less than skillful practice? What keeps me from founding friendships with others?*

*Shakyamuni Buddha*

# Day 26

**Another way that we can cultivate compassion is through the meditation practice of loving-kindness. It turns out that compassion, while innate, is also something that can be taught, learned and practiced.**

Kurland, Beth. "Beyond Empathy: The Power of Compassion." *Psychology Today*. 18 Sept. 2019. www.psychologytoday.com/us/blog/the-well-being-toolkit/201909/beyond-empathy-the-power-compassion.

*When was the last time I sat down and read the Karaniya Metta Sutta? What should be done "By one who is skilled in goodness, And who knows the path of peace?" What is gained by chanting the Karaniya Metta Sutta in Pali? What is gained by reading the Karaniya Metta Sutta in English or Sinhalese or some other language that I understand? How does meditation improve my Buddhist practice and quality of my life?*

*An Unexpected Guest*

## Day 27

**But it is important to press deeper, to recognize that hospitality is fundamental to the spiritual life. It is not only expressed in acts we perform and gifts we give — it is, more importantly, a state of mind. A generosity of spirit lies at the core of human hospitality, making hospitality the virtue which defines humanity itself.**

Siddiqui, Mona. "Divine Welcome: The Ethics of Hospitality in Islam and Christianity." *ABC Religion and Ethics.* 29 Jul. 2020. www.abc.net.au/religion/mona-siddiqui-hospitality-as-welcoming-in-gods-name/12503800.

*How is hospitality related to compassion? How does a generosity of spirit serve as a core to living a life of compassion? How does a generosity of spirit allow me to deal with unexpected guests or other interruptions? In what ways do I show hospitality to myself? My family and friends? My co-workers? The members of my spiritual community? To strangers I encounter? To others in my community, state, country, world?*

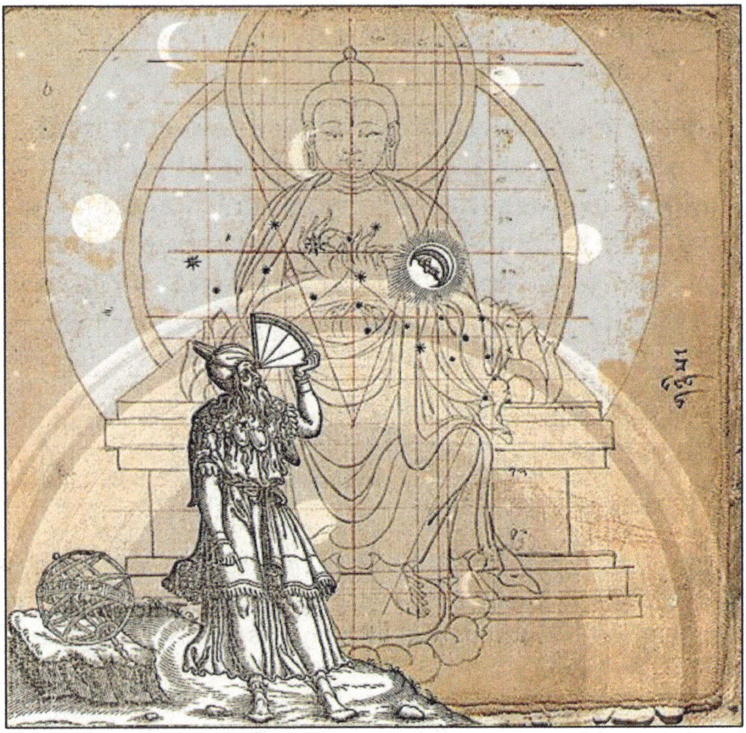

*Providing the Path*

# Day 28

**While it is not possible or advisable for an instructor to sit beside a student as they take a summative assessment, it is possible for an instructor to envision working alongside a student before, after, or perhaps even during a formative assessment.**

Akkaraju, Shylaja, et al. "Ensuring Student Success: Using Formative Assessment as the Key to Communication and Compassion Among Faculty, Students, and Staff." *New Directions for Community Colleges*, vol. 2019, no. 186, 2019, pp. 71-79. Academic Search Complete. DOI: 10.1002/cc.20358. p. 72.

*In what ways do I serve as an instructor to those around me such as my child, friends, and others with whom I come into contact? What does someone learn when they view the choices that I make in my life? How do I work with my "students" to ease their path toward Nibanna?*

*Lotus Emerging from Compost*

# Day 29

**As we advocate for change, it's essential that fierceness and tenderness be balanced. If we're too tender without taking enough fierce action, we may become complacent. But if our fierceness is not tempered with tenderness, we may become hostile and aggressive, undermining compassion.**

Neff, Kristen. "Four Ways Self Compassion Can Help You Fight for Social Justice." *Greater Good Magazine*. 14 Jun. 2021. greatergood.berkeley.edu/article/item/four_ways_self_compassion_can_help_you_fight_for_social_justice.

*Do I advocate for changes in laws, policies, or procedures that negatively impact individuals? How do I see such efforts on my part to be compassionate? Do I ever move to the extremes of fierceness, hostility, or aggression in advocating for compassionate changes? How do such extremes make it more difficult for me to achieve my goals? How can I act more tenderly toward myself and in trying to persuade others to make changes?*

# Next Steps

Until we reach Nibanna, there is always a next step.

After a month of considering the role of compassion in our lives, we should be more compassionate. But few of us would have become enlightened during the previous 30 days. We are not Arahants yet. Therefore, we will continue to reflect on the role of compassion in our lives as well as the other three Brahma Viharas: loving-kindness, equanimity, and sympathetic joy. We will continue to meditate, to read the *suttas*, and read Buddhist commentaries as well as other helpful materials.

As we end a month of reflection, we begin a new month of reflection, maybe not focused specifically on compassion but as individuals who are on the path to relieve *dukkha* or pervasive dissatisfaction, continued reflection is necessary.

*For Jackson*

# Day 30

**Once we see that the practice of the teaching does indeed bring peace, joy, and inner security in this very life, this will inspire our trust and confidence in the Dhamma as a whole, including those aspects that lie beyond our present capacity for personal verification.**

Bodhi, Bhikkhu. *In the Buddha's Words: An Anthology of Discourses from the Pali Canon*. Wisdom, 2005. p. 85.

*How does my experience allow me to trust the teachings found in the* Dhamma*? How does my experience with compassion make me want to act more compassionately toward myself and others? What are some of the next steps I want to take to improve my life as a compassionate individual?*

*Walking with Francis of Assisi*

# Day 31

**Attention leads to empathy, empathy leads to ethical reflection, and ethical reflection leads to activism to respond to suffering wherever we observe it.... Paying attention to the reality of suffering challenges us personally and politically to embody acts of healing and wholeness.**

Epperly, Bruce G. *Walking with Francis of Assisi: From Privilege to Activism*. Franciscan Media, 2021.p. 69.

*How do I respond to suffering when I observe it? What do I see as the ethical relationship between compassion and activism? How does the reality of suffering challenge me personally? How does the reality of suffering challenge me politically? What types of activism can I practice to act compassionately?*

# About
# Ehipassiko Press

Ehipassiko Press was started in June 2023 to publish Open Educational Resources (OERs) primarily in the fields of education, spirituality, and addiction recovery. We have since expanded our mission to include books that serve as reflective journals in a number of disciplines as well as to support student voices.

We hope that *Contemplating Compassion* will be the first in a series of "Contemplating ______" books that individuals can use for reflection and personal growth, not just in the Buddhist tradition. If you are interested in compiling a book for this series, please let us know.

Although we are not a Buddhist press, we extend the Buddhist tradition of not selling Dhamma to all our books. Therefore, our books are published with a Creative Commons license and are released online for free.

In the spirit of OERs and not selling Dhamma,

paperback editions of our books are offered through Amazon for cost of production. Neither our authors nor Ehipassiko Press receive royalties or other forms of compensation from our publications.

Please go to *ehipassikopress.org* for information about our other publications.

You may contact us at info@ehipassikopress.org.

Great Lakes
Buddhist Vihara
Center for Inner Peace & Meditation

## About the Great Lakes Buddhist Vihara

Established in 1997, the great Lakes Buddhist Vihara in Livonia, Michigan is a Buddhist Monastery in the Theravada Tradition. Even though the Vihara is modeled after a typical Sri Lankan temple and run by Buddhist monks who are trained and ordained in Sri Lanka, this is a venue for all who like to learn and practice Buddhism and meditation.

Our primary goal is to be a center for inner peace for all Buddhists and non-Buddhists in the Great Lakes area to practice the teachings of the Buddha. The activities we perform through mindfulness and loving-kindness way of life promote individual inner peace and social solidarity. These activities include offering Buddhist teachings for children and adults, meditation guidance, organizing volunteer projects for youth, and conducting religious ceremonies.

Website: https://glbvihara.org/.

## About the Author

Steven L. Berg is a professor of English and History at Schoolcraft College and is an active member of the Great Lakes Buddhist Vihara. He is the founder of Ehipassiko Press, LLC.

Dr. Berg is the author/editor of 16 books including *Addiction Recovery Through Buddhist Wisdom*. His other books range on subjects from addiction and recovery, quilting, research methodology, learning styles, and student transformation.

Although Dr. Berg describes himself as a research geek, his primary interest is working with and advocating for students. Through his work with Ehipassiko Press, he encourages self-reflection that leads to personal growth.

Made in the USA
Monee, IL
07 February 2025

11027233R00056